FLY FISH MINDSET

Work Less, Earn More, Catch Trout

Anthony Atwell, Jr.

www.flyfishmindset.com

First printing edition
2020

Copyright @ 2019 by Anthony Atwell, Jr.

All rights reserved. No part of this publication may be reproduced, distributed, or transmitted in any form or by any means, including photocopying, recording, or other electronic or mechanical methods, without the prior written permission of the publisher, except in the case of brief quotations embodied in critical reviews and certain other noncommercial uses permitted by copyright law. For permission requests, write to the publisher, addressed "Attention: Permissions Coordinator," at the address below.

ISBN: 978-0-578-59981-6 (Paperback)

Library of Congress Control Number: 2019919681

Front cover image by Reynaldo A. Licayan
Book design by Designer Reynaldo A. Licayan

Printed by KDP design

First Printing Edition 2020 - Fly Fish Mindset LLC - Anthony Atwell. Jr
6 Old Pecos Ct, Santa Fe, NM 87508

www.flyfishmindset.com

Fly Fish Mindset

Work Less, Earn More, Catch Trout

Anthony Atwell, Jr.

Why Fly Fish?
The Moment
On the Road Again
Solitude on the Water
Fishermen and Fisherwomen
Fishing with Family
The One that got Away
The Guide Life
Trout, Trucha, Trutta, Salmo
Equipment & Planning
Bugs & Entomology
Technique
Research & Preparation
Go Fly Fish Now
Recommendations
References
Fly Fishing Adventures

Fly Fish Bucket List

Why fly fish?

Catching a a three-pound brown with a five weight Sage rod is just as exciting as landing a 150-pound Belize tarpon on a streamer.

It's good to laugh with your friends.

Extracting from the daily race and easing into the flow of nature brings a feeling of peace and wholeness.

I love fly fishing. It is an informed process where with every cast I learn something new about the fish and the environment. I feel energized and aware, in touch with myself and the world around me. Fly fishing is about choices. You get out there, interpret the environment, and make educated guesses. Like most of life, fishing is great fun when your choices are correct and a challenge when they're not. Over the course of many years on the water, I've learned to think like a fish. With a tuned-in fly fish mindset, I have a calm and focused approach to other parts of my life.

    I turn sixty years old this year and first picked up a fishing rod at age seven. I've enjoyed fifty-three years (and counting) of the fishing life and it is an honor to share this story with all the people that love to fish and all those yet to fish. I encourage the old fisher boys out there to embrace the basics and to the newbies, start simple and take it in stride.

    Break clear of your routine and get out on the water. Bring your kids, grandkids, neighbors, and friends to the call of the rivers and outdoor adventure. Even without a single bite, there is inspiration in the water and we are inexorably connected to it. A trout's home is ultimately our home.

    I want to thank all the people in my life who made fishing important to me – My dad Anthony , my son Alexander , my cousin Billy Atwell, and my best, oldest friend George Lee.

Viva La Pura Vida – Live the Good Life
Anthony Atwell, Jr.

THE MOMENT

Memories— catching my first perch on a cane pole, pulling in a monster bass fishing a purple worm, pulling in a trot line with forty fish, snakes, and a seven-foot white catfish. Fishing has held an indelible place in my life since childhood and I wouldn't have it any other way.

    I fly fished for the first time at age fourteen on Colorado's Gunnison River but the trip started at a fly fish outfitters shop. I had my entire savings to spend; twenty dollars eating a hole in my pocket. I was, well, like a kid in a candy store but instead of jelly beans and licorice I picked out colorful flies. The sales clerk quickly pointed out five flies for twenty bucks. I mumbled something about that seemed expensive, so he gave me one fly for free. My dad bought my Colorado fishing license, leader, and a small fly rod and reel on sale. I beamed like the bright morning sun as we walked out of the store and loaded our loot into the car. I was going trout fishing for the first time with my dad and new gear! I checked my box of flies; some had wings and others looked like the ordinary black flies we had swarming around our heads all summer. The sales clerk told me to fish a 'dry and a dropper.' I wasn't completely sure what that meant but it sounded wonderful and I couldn't wait to get to the river.

     We drive down canyon from Lake City and quickly found a spot with easy access to the Gunnison. The Gunnison is a mighty big river, especially when you're fourteen and have never seen a Colorado freestone river. And it roared like a freight train, with furious frothy green rage slapping against boulders here, and oddly quiet and tranquil eddy pools there. The morning was cool and clear and I felt the moisture in the air and when I walked past low shrubs the dew left temporary art patterns on my jeans. All around me was green forest and weathered gray boulders, with a cloudless, impossibly blue sky above my head. Dad helped me rig the rod, using unfamiliar words like line, tippet, and midge. I did not really understand trout lingo, but paid close attention to his sage advice about casting a fly rod. This was only his second fly fishing trip but to me he was a wise and seasoned veteran.

     This was nothing like bass fishing in my old hometown in Texas. My first few casts were terrible and the harder I tried, the worse it got. Several casts hooked into the nearby grass and I became increasingly frustrated. Looking on nearby, Dad said, "Remember casting lesson number one—go 10 to 2 and easy does it." That took about twenty repetitions, several more false casts and another grass snag; but I got the hang of it and haven't put down a fly rod since. I caught three brown trout that morning. They averaged about twelve inches apiece but looked enormous to me and it was only by good fortune that I caught them in the first place. I had slack in the line all morning and one "catch" involved hauling in the line by hand and dragging a poor trout onto the bank. Dad watched this all unfold and his happiness in the moment was infectious. We laughed and learned a lot that day, sharing a special time in our lives.

On the Road Again

A tradition with nearly the same reverence as fishing itself is the road trip. Saddling up, if you will, with a load of gear and jittery anticipation and ready to drive one hour or ten to your favorite fly fish adventure grounds.

We trout bums from Santa Fe tend to gravitate north, up to the Rio Chama or San Juan. Roll just another hour north of Chama is Colorado and a trio of legendary fishing rivers—the Conejos, Upper Rio Grande, and the mighty Arkansas. The drive north is relaxing and we never tire of the rugged scenery and the unmistakable landscapes of unique freestone river basins, each with its own supporting cast of lakes, ponds, and tributary streams.

Naturally, any respectable road trip requires a healthy quantity of provisions loaded into a cooler packed with ice—beer, water, apples, granola, ham sandwiches on rye with Dijon mustard, Fritos, more beer, and sometimes wine, depending on the crowd assembled.

Off-season the cruising is easy, with wide open roads matching the big sky above. On-season trips are a different story, of course, and are more about slowing down and going with the flow. Enormous RVs, parades of motorcycles, and road work is the name of the game in the warmer months.

We listen to Willie Nelson and the Grateful Dead and Garth Brooks when the old radio works, and hear songs about sunsets and sunrises, and the stars and moon, while driving through it all in real time. It's a classic country western song in motion.

We don't hear many songs about fly fishing for rainbow trout, but that's okay. My buddies have enough fish stories to keep me entertained. And telling a fish story is an art form, for those unfamiliar with the tradition. A great fishing story is like walking a tightrope between exaggerated truth and embellished white lies. The longer folks listen to your fantastic tale, the more likely they will believe you hook, line, and sinker.

But in today's age of cell phones and cameras, you better have proof to back up your story. If you don't have photos, I suggest buying everyone numerous beers and then performing animated fish charades. You're guaranteed a few laughs even if nobody believes your story.

We always stop at the local café in Antonito, Colorado; where they have strong coffee and coconut cream pie. Inside we always find a few like-minded fishermen, almost always dressed in the same outfits of plaid shirts and waders. Conversation turns lively when someone asks who caught the biggest trout this trip and the fish tales get taller by the minutes.

Fueled from the café stop, we gain momentum for that first cast on Costilla Creek, three hours north of Santa Fe. Costilla Creek meanders through grassy meadows of blooming flowers. The river flows at an easygoing 70 cubic feet per second and is perfect for wading out to cast. A few bighorn sheep watched me cast the hours away, nymph and egg fishing for rainbows. One native beauty jumped four times and I caught a bunch from 12"-16". After the excitement on the water it's time to set up camp.

The best part about camping here is being next to the sounds of the river, wildlife of various sizes moving about, and a forest of enormous Ponderosa pine and spruce peppered with aspen. I took a break from the river at midday to avoid the heat, ate a big lunch, and grabbed a nap.

That evening, we gathered wood for a campfire and enjoyed a hearty meal—venison sausage from my last deer hunt, Southwest salad, and mashed potatoes; all topped off with lemon wedges and fresh strawberries with honey.

With full bellies, the river's lullaby sings me to sleep and dreams of lots of trout.

Solitude on the Water

Time on the water is different than what passes on land. On the water is peace, reflection on the past, wonder of the future, and most of all, comfort in the present. It is awareness of exploration versus expectation and a place to escape mental boxes.

I am on the Pecos River, up by Cowles, New Mexico. Watching the river's inexorable flow downstream, I realize change is the only constant in life and time past cannot be regained. It is a reminder to live the now and the message is there in the wind through the aspens and pines, in birdsong, and the flow of the river. With an ocean of sounds around me, I touch the water and feel its energy and know I am part of a greater whole.

I watch the river move and can almost feel the trout holding along the seam of slow and faster waters. Time slows and in the synergy where one bug finds one trout, I feel content no matter the outcome. There, a splash on the water; most likely a rainbow harvesting a spring stonefly. There is a rhythm and I look up to see the day's first hatch of stone flies above my head.

My heart beats faster, knowing the trout sense the oncoming feast. Channeling my best instincts and observations, I quickly tie on a 16 brown stonefly and 22 black silver-striped midge. I set my indicator four feet above the flies and will adjust my depth as needed with weighted putty.

I walk slowly to the edge of a small pool and see the trout rising halfway and then disappearing below. That means they are feeding just below the surface, so I shorten my indicator a bit and excitedly lob my first casts along the edge of the pool. On the third cast the bite was about three feet off the grass bank. The fight was on, with my three-weight Sage rod seeing the business end of the action. The rod bent halfway over and there was no time to haul in the fish; best to let it run and tucker out. After about four minutes of playing the trout, I landed my first rainbow of the day. She was about twenty inches and every one of them beautiful as the day around me.

Quickly I remove the midge and revive the rainbow in the current, cradling her beneath her belly and behind the lower dorsal fins, while gently holding the tail in my other hand. About ten seconds later, she slowly slides out of my hand and meanders back into the pool. It is an unforgettable moment of receiving and giving back, a moment just as poignant as the one before and those to come.

Fishermen & Fisherwomen

At some point in their lives, fly fishermen and fisherwomen realize there is something special for them out there. Yes, we need to provide for ourselves, family, and community; but what else gives us love and satisfaction? My growing appreciation today is to treasure God's creations, work less, earn more, and go fishing. I've also developed a keen awareness of some of the differences between fishing genders.

Fisherwomen tend to have the advantage in fly fishing. They are often more patient than men and pay close attention to detail; two essential qualities to fly fishing. They also have a softer touch and can usually thread the tippet through a #26 fly in a snap.

You can learn a lot from watching fisherwomen on the river. They move slower and watch their step, naturally aware of the smells and sounds of nature around them. Interestingly, I've found that many women listen closely to men's sage fishing advice and then head right out and catch the first and largest trout of the day, while on the other side of the river is a man pouting because he did not heed his own advice.

Fisherwomen also understand that when the water is clear, it's important to sneak up gradually or risk scaring the smartest, biggest fish. They understand that monster brown trout grow to twenty-six inches because they are on the lookout for people and predator birds and know you're coming long before you get there.

I always enjoy watching a gal mastering the cast too. At first, it's like everyone else's "bass cast", but given a few visual examples of a slower cast, the ladies quickly become very adept. Once she understands a bit more line out makes for an easier cast, then it is all about reading the water and setting up drift.

My girlfriend Renee is an ideal example. After a ten-minute lesson on the overhead cast, drift and mend, she presented nymphs with the flow of the current and tempo of bugs in the water. Several fishing trips later, Renee showed confidence using a roll cast in the wind and high-sticking around boulders.

Patience is truly a virtue with flyfishing. Fisherwomen will stay in one spot and fish it until the cows come home. Sometimes that's good when trout are biting; but usually one will catch more trout by patiently working a hole, then moving on if there is no action. Working more water and keeping your line in the water at the right depth and with the right flies produces more strikes.

I remember one smart trout, in a determined effort to escape the net, swam between Renee's legs and wiggled a ways up her waders. She howled like a coyote under the full moon and I am very sure that trout broke his tippet and swam away.

Now it's the men's turn. We all want to catch more truchas (trout) so we all get a turn in the hot seat. To start, everything I said about fisherwomen also applies to fishermen. That also means to experienced fishermen who "know everything" about fishing, but not much about fly fishing. Even I have to admit I know enough about fly fishing to get me into trouble with my fishing audience.

Fishermen are often all about adventure. They figure the harder it is to access the water, the likelier it is they'll find bigger fish. And the story sounds better if you had to trudge through salt cedar swamplands, fending off ravenous insects burrowing into your bearded face and the smallest target of bare skin.

Fishermen love their fly fishing gear too. I mean they really love it; all that gear is like a mobile man cave and the more gear the better, even if he has no idea how to use it. However, in fly fishing, sometimes less is more. Take rod lengths, for example. Do you really want to use your ten-foot Orvis six weight rod on a small river with lots of brush, or would you prefer a six-foot Sage three weight?

Gentlemen, don't get trapped in the little pickle syndrome. Bigger is not better when fly fishing, especially when it comes to choosing the size of your flies. I know guys who prefer tying on larger flies because they are easier to see and handle, but think about what lives in the river. Make a compromise for best results, such as testing larger caddis on top of your rig and tiny midges below your caddis. If you see surface action, setup a stimulator and emerging caddis.

Fishermen also tend to plow into the river in a noisy eruption of splashes and turbulence without stopping to note what the fish are doing that day. They might even miss the fact that the trout swam away with all the ruckus of their grand entrance of ripples and scraping of rocks and clanging of gear. It's important to learn to ease up on fishable water.

And once on the water, be smart. When fishermen fall in a river, it's often because they opted against bringing a walking staff because "those are for old guys." Well, that train of thought will turn you into an injured man who can't fish anymore.

I grade falls from one to five. A level one fall is like having a yank in your back and getting your shirt a little wet. Falling at level five includes submerging under frigid water, hitting the rocks while bruising your hands and butt, and your waders fill up with cold water because you forgot to put your wader belt on. It's lucky you didn't remain submerged and dragged away in the current. And good thing your buddy was there to drag you out of the water and recover. Yes, this was yours truly on the San Juan River about twenty years ago and I learned a hard lesson that day.

The fact is your slippery boots need some metal wedges, you need to slow down your movements in the water, and use a walking staff for stability.

FISHING WITH FAMILY

I am very proud of my son Alex. He is in great shape and can outwalk and outski me these days but I remind him that I taught him to walk and ski, and I am still teaching him the nuances of fly fishing.

Persistence best describes Alex when he fishes. He never gives up and he will fish thirty holes some days, even if the fish are not biting. That is an excellent mindset but I make sure to tell him that a sound fly fish philosophy includes varying lure insects, depending on what conditions tell him. And sometimes just watching who is catching fish on which fly at what depth is all you need to change your fishing luck.

I am a dad, just like other dads, who want to see their children grow up having fun and leave their cell phones behind. There's something special about being outside that inspires a feeling of happiness and a time to share and catch wild trout.

For me, it's great fun watching a beginning fly fisher evolve from an aggressive bass cast to a slower, rhythmic action with a fly rod. When I teach beginners, we use a shorter rod, smaller leader, and cast only with a moderate amount of line. I stress the fundamentals—allow the flies to float naturally with the current and mend your line from time to time so it does not drag the fly or the indicator. Kids will generally hear you for about twenty seconds and apply the technique correctly. Then you return fifteen minutes later to watch them fish their way, pulling the fish onto the bank with great pride.

Dads are great about teaching life lessons too. Fishing dads, in particular, will take the time to show kids how to cradle the fish, return him to water, and revive him; teaching the importance of preserving a fish so he can grow bigger and reproduce to continue the circle of fish, catch, release, and fish again. There is also something to be said in favor of allowing another fisherman the joy of catching the same fish.

It's even more fun to see kids' excited faces as a trout takes the bait and runs with the line. I try to teach new fly fishers not to hold a death grip on the line and yank the bait out of the trout's mouth. On average it seems, beginners will land the biggest trout of the day, and overall land about twenty percent of the fish that bite. Such is the trout fishing learning curve.

The One that got Away

I have to laugh when I think about all the fish that got away. But when I am in the moment, on the water, and the fish escapes, it's not as funny.

Even professional trout guides lose fish. Just last week I had the privilege of fishing with Pat Blankenship, owner of Conejos River Anglers in Colorado. Initially Pat hooked three healthy rainbows in a row, until the big dog brown trout taught him some fish etiquette.

Pat was fishing a 16 rainbow midge and 22 black midge, along with a bit of weighted putty. Depth of the nymphs was approximately four feet, where Pat thought the column of trout were feeding. There was a bend in the river, where rapids water ran over rocks and into a pool at the base of a small cliff. It was a veritable fish feed bin here, with nymphs and emergers feeding the pool constantly.

Pat was casting into the rapids and allowing his bait to flow into the pool. This was the correct strategy versus casting directly into the pool and possibly spooking the big fish. On one particular cast, Pat was solid on his presentation until a huge brown trout grabbed the bait and ran downstream.

The fish struck the emerger and ran out about thirty yards in about ten seconds. I could hear the high pitched whine of the reel and line running off the rod. The strike was instantaneous and I saw Pat only had time to set the hook in a cockeyed upstream motion. Most river guides will tell you to always set the hook downstream but Pat simply didn't have a chance.

I didn't think this was going to end well for Pat; the big kahuna brown had the upper hand. A tight line was no problem for Pat and in good form, he held his rod tip high and let it do most of the work keeping tension on the fish. The problem was the senior brown trout sat on the other side of a roaring spring current among a pile of rocks.

Several minutes passed and Mr. Brown refused to budge behind the rocks. The stalemate was not looking good until another run began, this time straight back toward Pat. Forty years of fishing experience came into play, Pat furiously stripping his line in, attempting to keep some sort of tension. I heard a litany of groans and damnations as the situation devolved from professional, in-control fly fisherman to massive brown trout running the show. In just a matter of seconds the finale was upon us.

Ten feet in front of Pat, Mr. Brown leaped out of the water in a fury of acrobatic arches and twists. Pat stared wide-eyed at the drama as the fish seemed to look him right in eye, then spit out the emerger and plunge back into the depths of the river pool.

Silence followed as we bowed our heads in reverence to the fish gods, humble that we lost another kahuna trout. But this is okay; we realize if we did not lose some fish some of the time, there would be nothing to learn from and it is most definitely not as much fun. Indeed, the one that got away is an important fact of life.

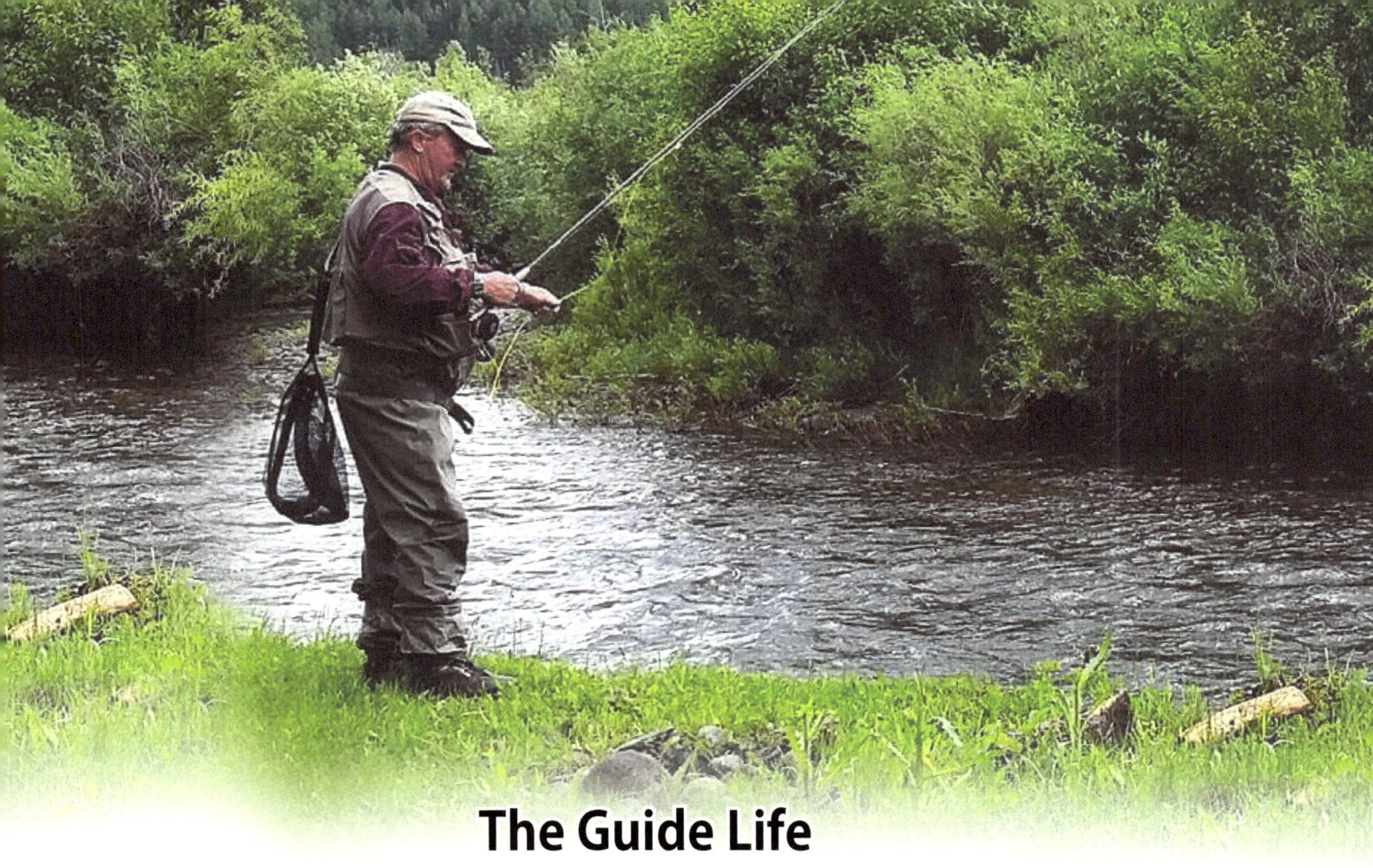

The Guide Life

Fishing guides come in all shapes and colors. And they communicate through a strange language, "trout speak", which allows them to convey the who, what, where, and why trout are biting today.

"Clean the salad…..death grip……..4x tippet versus 6x tippet….the weather…….kahuna……dog fish…… he is a runner…..she is a diver….FIF-faith in fishing………set the hook!…give to the king……get his head up………. strip it in faster….hittin on Drakes……bit the stimulator….high stick drift with a hopper…..daddy long legs…… nippers…..riffles……"

Expert guides fish the season for clients and then fish offseason for themselves. They know their water year round. Next time you get a chance, watch a good guide move around his riparian environment. He moves methodically, pausing occasionally to study an insect, always looking all around, above and below, sensing the river's pulse.

Professional guides understand everything about their gear. They continually study their profession and learn from associate guides, gear suppliers, and their clients. They keep many rods and reels for varied trout habitat, and know when to use the correct rod, not "the favorite" one. Supporting it all are a dozen boxes of flies, terrestrials and streamers.

The best guides have a practiced and elegant skill to cast and can pass on simple ways of teaching you great casting as well. A great guide will cast within an inch of his target ninety-nine percent of the time, making his cast look effortless after thousands of casts in all conditions.

Expert guides are very adept with knots, too, and can tie at least five types of knots in ten seconds or less. When instructing those new to the craft, guides prefer to tie your flies on because they know their knots will hold under most conditions, while many "newbie" knots will slip loose because rookie fly fishers generally do not practice their knots at home before hitting the river.

Guides are also very good at telling stories, which they comfortably leverage into teaching tools. They will tell you all about their clients, why this one caught large browns while the other kept missing the hook set. If you share some of your fish stories, I promise you will get an earful of fly fishing lore all day long. Take notes and shoot some photos or videos. You will learn a lot, but it will take time to fully absorb all the tips and trivia.

My Tesuque Pueblo friend and trout guide, Mark Swazo, gives prayer and blessings before we fish. Facing east, he sprinkles cornmeal and blesses the earth, water, sky, and all things outside these dimensions. He blesses the fish and asks the fish gods for blessings of a good catch. He conveys his gratitude for being here in the greater universe by offering the cornmeal. This greater awareness helps to assure a good catch and release. Our latest blessing saw Mark and I catch and release around fifty trout from the tiny Cimmaron River in Northern New Mexico—a true fish story if there ever was.

The Fish

Trout, Trucha, Trutta, Salmo

Every time I catch a trout, I take a good look at markings and colors. It's amazing to see the wide variety from stream to river to lake and I am forever fascinated to know that trout have been around a long time, evolving over millions of years. I often wonder if trout and people will be around in a million more years? How will we evolve?

Trout have evolved into unique species around the world, including China, Japan, Africa, Slovenia, Turkey, Azerbaijan, Norway, Iceland, Europe, Canada, and the United States. Many trout live in fresh water and sea water, and are known as anadromous (sea-run). Other trout are freshwater only.

Scientific names are curious to note: Oncorynchuss mykiss (Rainbowtrout), Salmo trutta fario, Salmo ohridana, Salmo trutta aralensis, Salvelinus boganidae, Salvethymus svetovidovi. In New Mexico and Colorado trout include rainbows, cutbows, browns, cut throats, and brookies.

Oncorynchuss mykiss, rainbow trout, was named by German naturalist and taxonomist Johann Julius Walbaum in 1792. He based the name on specimens from the Kamchatka Peninsula, Russia, where the name used for fish is mykizha.

In general, adult stream rainbow trout average between one to five pounds, while lake trout grow to as much as twenty pounds. Coloration varies by species, but most adult fish have a reddish stripe along the lateral line.

Breeding time for rainbow trout normally occurs early to late spring; for brown trout in the fall. However, high winter runoff can affect the timing of all trout hatches.

Trout are fussy creatures, choosing cold, aerated water at preferred temperatures of forty to sixty degrees. Trout are found in rivers, streams, ponds and lakes, and each environment requires a different fishing strategy.

Around New Mexico and Southern Colorado I ask, "Donde estan las truchas?" Where are the trout? I casually inquire at local cafes, gas stations, and fly shops because the locals know all about the best locations. Buy them a cup of coffee and pie and the secrets will come forth.

But where will you find trout, if you do not see trout? One of my favorite guides, Curtis Moore, said "Look for the edges – edges of river or lake, where slow water meets faster water, where shallow meets deep, where water meets rock edges, where shadow meets light."

Yesterday I visited the Pecos River, about thirty minutes from Santa Fe. It was a special May afternoon as the leaves were blooming and the temperature was a perfect sixty degrees. Late spring snow runoff continued and the river chugged along at 450 CFS. That's a lot of water for a small river, so I chose to fish the shallows where there is lesser current and a chance for fish to feed. Water clarity had improved from my last visit weeks ago, though it was still cloudy but bottom visible about three feet down.

I always hang out by the water before I start fishing. I find my fishing is more productive when I rig up at the river and I know what my fishing research says for recommended flies. I also know what my senses tell me once I am on the river.

Looking around with polarized sunglasses, I search for activity below the water, on the water, around the water. I listen to the river and the river's riparian environment. I try and see like the trout in their favorite habitats. Think like a fish—what is the easiest way to get a meal without moving too much?

Then I run through my fly fish mental checklist:
Is the water clear or cloudy?
Is the river high or low?
Water temperature?
How windy is it now or will it be?
What bugs are in the riparian brush next to the river?
What bugs are in the water, above and below the area I want to fish?
What are the birds and animals up to?
What time of day is it? Where is the sun on the water?
How is the river flowing; slow bends and pools or fast moving and rocks?
Can I cast both sides of my body, or do I prefer one side of the river?
Can I fish the middle of the river and cross the river safely?
Where will I fish?
Where are the fish rising?
What is plan A, plan B, plan C to catch and release my trout?

Then I enter the river and kick up a few rocks in the shallows and sein for bugs underneath. From what bugs I identify in and around the water, I select a suitable fly imitation and unfurl the first cast.

EQUIPMENT & SETUP

There is nothing worse than driving for hours in the middle of the mountains and realize you forgot one special fly and your guide's name and phone number. There is no internet or wifi connection around and you realize how screwed this makes things. Less time on the water equals less fish.

Think about your fishing objective before the trip. Ask yourself, will I really use this or need this extra item if something breaks? Am I willing to travel with it?

Checklists are a great way of preparing for a great fishing trip. Here are some tried and true checklist items I use:
- Days on the road
- Location and contacts
- Weather
- Maps
- Emergency contacts, home security, credit card notification
- Personal gear
— Cell phone and chargers for auto/computer and wall outlet, toiletries and meds, TP, extra glasses and sunglasses, sunscreen, inner and outer clothing appropriate to weather and number of days of the road, boots, sandals. How do I stay dry but not over heated? If I get wet and cold, what is my plan B?

- Fishing gear
— Take what you must, based on your area research. Take extra gear in case something breaks. Usually you do not have access to replacement gear when you need it most.

Create a written check list: rods, reels, lines, leaders, tippets, weights, flies and streamers....flashlight, knives, pliers, screwdriver, large Ziploc bags, fish net, bug sein, bear spray, sunscreen, bug spray, fishing license and area permits, water bottle full of water, snack bars, wide brim hat, polarized glasses, wind/rain gear, fishing vest/sling pack to stow this gear, boots, waders, walking/wading stick, first aid kit, and of course toilet paper. Pack this all in one rolling duffel bag. Initial all your gear, tag your bags, leave your card inside a bag and vest (This is a big help if lost or misplaced in transit.)

Make sure gear is clean and in working order. Clean those fishing lines and reels and watch your casts fly smoothly.

- RV Gear, camping gear or motel gear
—Take your favorite coffee and filters, cooler/ice, snacks, libations, et al. Hit the grocery on the way to your destination. Depending on your accommodations, make sure to bring the appropriate gear and spare parts.

Decide on how your gear is stowed and how you prefer to travel. I recommend a duffel bag with rollers, large enough to store your rod tubes and other equipment. Try using one bag and one backpack. Double check your gear before you leave.

Finally, have your vehicle and trailer checked for basic maintenance before departure. Be sure to let your emergency contacts know when and where you are traveling.

BUGS & ENTOMOLOGY

Sometimes I look into my fly box and feel overwhelmed. My little fish brain is on overload and I cannot pick that perfect combination of flies. Stonefly, mayfly, caddisfly, damselfly, midge, emerger, nymph—it's enough to drive you crazy. Then you look in your other fly box to find stimulators, ants, beetles, other unknown terrestrials, and some worn streamers. Where do I start?

I long ago found that it is best for me to observe and assess the trout's environment as I go. Fly fishing requires you to scope out an environment and then develop a strategy for bugs and presentation. Think like a trout; imagine how a trout picks its food.

It's always a good idea to watch bug movement on and over the water. Activity changes hourly, so keep your eyes open. You need to look up twenty feet in the air because hatches often start high and move down toward the water. It could be mayflies, or ant flies, or blue wing olives; and activity will vary from stream to stream and time of year.

Then check what's happening in the water. Serious fly fishermen use a sein attached to their net. They kick up some rocks above and below the area they want to fish, and sein for the bugs released into the water. Then they examine their catch with a magnifying glasses and note details such as form, sizes and coloration. With a solid assessment of the bugs, find similar matches in your fly box.

Take it a step further and identify your local bug population's entomology. I recommend taking a short entomology course from troutsflyfishing.com and signing up for their newsletter. Entomology has helped me identify the bugs fish are feeding on, and then match the same or similar bug in my fly box.

Keep in mind that trout are feeding machines in their home environments. Different water, different days, different bugs. What bugs do you see in the air, under plant leaves, and when you sein the water? Are the insects adult, emergers, or nymphs? Are they large or small? What insect colors and natural tones do you see? How can your fly box mimic the insects trout are feeding on?

Remember that most trout feeding goes on under the water, usually closer to the bank. In this case we are talking about fishing midges, emergers, larvae, eggs, terrestrials and streamers. Usually I will start out with a dry fly and wet fly. In Colorado I can legally fish a dry and two droppers, unless in special waters. I tend to begin with a longer rig and longer bug separation; that way I can adjust downsize if needed, or use an adjustable indicator on the line.

It's all about finding the depth where fish are feeding. Most trout folks around Southern Colorado use a seven foot leader, 4-5x tippet, bug separation three to four feet dry to dropper, and 1-2 feet between droppers.

If this lingo is driving you nuts, it's best to hire a guide several times to show you the ropes while having some fun catching fish. The rest will come with time.

Keep thinking like a trout. Is it a sunny day or a grey day? Before I choose my flies, I tend to follow old school fly fishing advice—use colorful patterns on bright days and dark colors on grey days. Cloudy days usually require a darker pattern for contrast in the water. If trout will not bite, switch strategies and test the opposite.

The size of your flies is a big deal as well. Just because you are on a big river does not mean trout are feeding on your newest granddaddy purple long legs #8.

Keep Learning, Keep Reading, Keep Fishing—and see references in the back of this book.

TECHNIQUE

I finally realized you have to think like a trout in order to catch a trout.

Thinking like a trout means many things to a fly fisherman or fisherwoman, like water temp, water depth, water flow, water clarity, time of season, time of day, insect activity, entomology, presentation, setting the hook, retrieval, netting, handling, and release. It's a lot to understand, so start simple.

Internet resources and YouTube are full of fly fishing videos. Check out fly casting techniques to start. After watching, go and practice in your yard or nearest body of water. Practice casting with a leader and fly on the water and without fly over the grass. Feel the timing and body position of a proper cast. Set a target and practice your accuracy from different distances. Feel your body positioning transition as you make the cast.

Also be sure to practice tying your fly knots before hitting the river. I preach this because when you are standing in the current and in the wind; you want to know you can tie on your fly quickly and securely. Hot tip:

do not drink too much coffee before tying knots and threading tiny eyelets! It's not easy with shaking hands and wear magnifying glasses if you need to.

When practicing fly fishing with a mentor or fishing guide, you will learn more fly fishing technique faster. Remember that the local boys understand their river day in and day out, in all weather and water conditions. When I start fishing a new river drainage, I choose a local guide who grew up in the area. This speeds up my fly fish mindset and allows me to catch more trout.

Messing up your fly cast while practicing is fine. Messing up your fly cast and hooking the nearest tree while fishing the honey hole is not fine. I remember one bad cast I had, the lure went straight into my brother's head and embedded there. Dad had to take him to the hospital to remove the barbed hook. In the meantime the guide took me back to the boat and made me cast many times until I was sure my casting line cleared the boat and passengers. He reminded me to always wear a hat and sunglasses to protect myself from bad casts and uncontrolled retrievals, and I never forgot the lessons from that day.

Hot tip #2: Clean off your Salad—after a few casts, clean off the moss and other foliage stuck on your flies. No trout wants to eat a dirty fly.

Fisherwomen and Fishermen need to remember, trout often feed in the shallowest water, so start your casting on the edges first, then gradually cast further out.

RESEARCH AND PREPARATION

I use a variety of internet resources and my fishing library before taking a trip. It's good to study area fishing guide reports, USGS water flows, and other fisherman comments. Before venturing into the wild, I also want to understand the river flow conditions, flies and terrestrials of the week, and weather conditions.

I stir this pot of information and create a plan of attack. Quality fly fishing time is precious on the river, so I want to be organized and ready to go. Once those bugs start hatching, you want to start casting. After all, you can't catch a trout unless the fly is in the water.

I check my vest for all the property tools of the trade—tippets, weight, floatant, indicators, sunscreen, polarized sunglasses, clippers, fish pliers, bug sein, fish license. Then I check my fly boxes for the correct types of flies in various sizes and colors recommended that month, for that river. When I say flies I mean dry flies, wet flies, nymphs, puppa, terrestrials, and streamers.

Clothing can be a tricky proposition in early spring. At eight thousand feet, weather changes fast. I always stick my gear in one duffle bag, including thermal socks, rain gear, wind gear, tshirts, caps, waders, boots, walking staff, and net.

For the Conejos River I choose my Sage nine foot rod, five-weight line, and 5x tippet. Any lighter tackle and I might lose that twenty-five inch Rainbow. It's early spring and the trout are spawning. Runoff just starting on the Conejos River in Southern Colorado. Water clarity still about five feet, so fish ought to be active.

From 9 AM to noon it's great, hitting black and red beadhead nymphs about three feet under. Then it started sleeting. My truck is a thirty-minute walk, so I can sit it out, fish, or walk back. I decided to keep moving and stay warm. I lined up a white and green streamer, about two feet apart. I figure one of my streamers will hit the right column where the fish feed beneath the sleet.

Twenty minutes into this messy situation my attention turns on as my Sage rod bends, almost yanking the rod out of my hand. Next thing I know, this bwana trout races downstream and I dare not grab my line in the infamous death grip. My heart is pounding, pulse racing; good thing I have a solid stance and the reel drag is working. The dance changes about thirty yards out as bwana trout turns toward me and I start stripping line like a bat outta hell. I get lucky and regain line tension.

After what seems like a thirty-minute fight, the brownie begins to nose up, signaling he is tiring. I know better;at the first sight of my net, the fish will run. I stay patient a few more minutes, making sure he tires. It proves to be a good strategy as I ease him into the net, leaving him in the water while I quickly unhook the white streamer. The trout is about twenty-four inches and so fat it's hard to hold him; a beautiful creature indeed. I ease him into the current and off he swims, until we meet again.

Fly Fish Mind

GO FLY FISH NOW

I turned 60 this year but I'm still the same good ol' Texas boy who loves the great outdoors and Mother Nature's playful hand. When I moved to Santa Fe, New Mexico about thirty-five years ago, I switched to fly fishing realizing how satisfying it is to "go with flow".

I remember being asked to attend a wedding with two weeks fishing left in the season. It wasn't really a contest; I didn't go to the wedding. I have been paying for that decision ever since, but I caught three fine browns that trip and I have no regrets.

Remember that fly fishing involves a process of ongoing learning; an awakening that every body of water is unique, that every day offers variety and choices. Over time, you start to think like a fish thinks. You learn that catching that fish is much more than a cool-looking fly on your rig.

I urge people to realize the waters and habitat of trout are the source of our water too. We must protect it, keep it clean, and return most of your catch to the water. This is the natural cycle of life. Breaking the cycle breaks the environment that sustains us.

Be sure to check out the fly fishing resources noted. Fly fishing knowledge makes for great fishing—what you learn from great fishing makes for great living.

For those who enjoy fly fishing and traveling first class, contact me to discuss customized fishing tours.

See you on the water.
Regards, Anthony

RECOMMENDATIONS

FAVORITE FLY FISH WATER	–	5hrs or less from Santa Fe, NM
New Mexico Rivers North	–	San Juan River, Rio Costilla, East Fork Jemez River, Los Pinos River, Rio Chama
New Mexico Lakes North	–	Fenton Lake, Santa Cruz Reservoir, Navajo Reservoir, Abiquiu Reservoir, Canijon Lakes
Colorado Rivers South	–	Conejos River, Rio Grande River, Arkansas River, Gunnison River, Rio Grande, Animas River
Recommended Flies for most rivers and creeks	–	Northern New Mexico, South Central Colorado

Pheasant Tail Nymph, Elk Hair Caddis, Light Cahill, Royal Wulff, Gold Ribbed Hare's Ear Nymph, Griffith's Gnat, Woolly Bugger, Blue Winged Olive, Prince Nymph, Parachute Adams, Emergent Sparkle Pupa, San Juan Worm

Fly Fish Mindset

REFERENCES

- Wikipedia.com
- The Little Red Book of Fly Fishing, Deeter and Meyers
- The History of Fly Fishing in Fifty Flies, Ian Whitelaw
- Rocky Mountain Angling Club
- Google Maps
- Trout of the World, James Prosek
- Fifty Places to Fly Fish Before You Die, Chris Santella

- Troutsflyfishing.com
- Pocket Guide to Fly Fishing, Ron Cordes
- All Fishermen Are Liars, John Gierach
- New Mexico Game and Fish
- Colorado Game and Fish
- Trout Unlimited
- The Fly Fish Journal
- The Drake

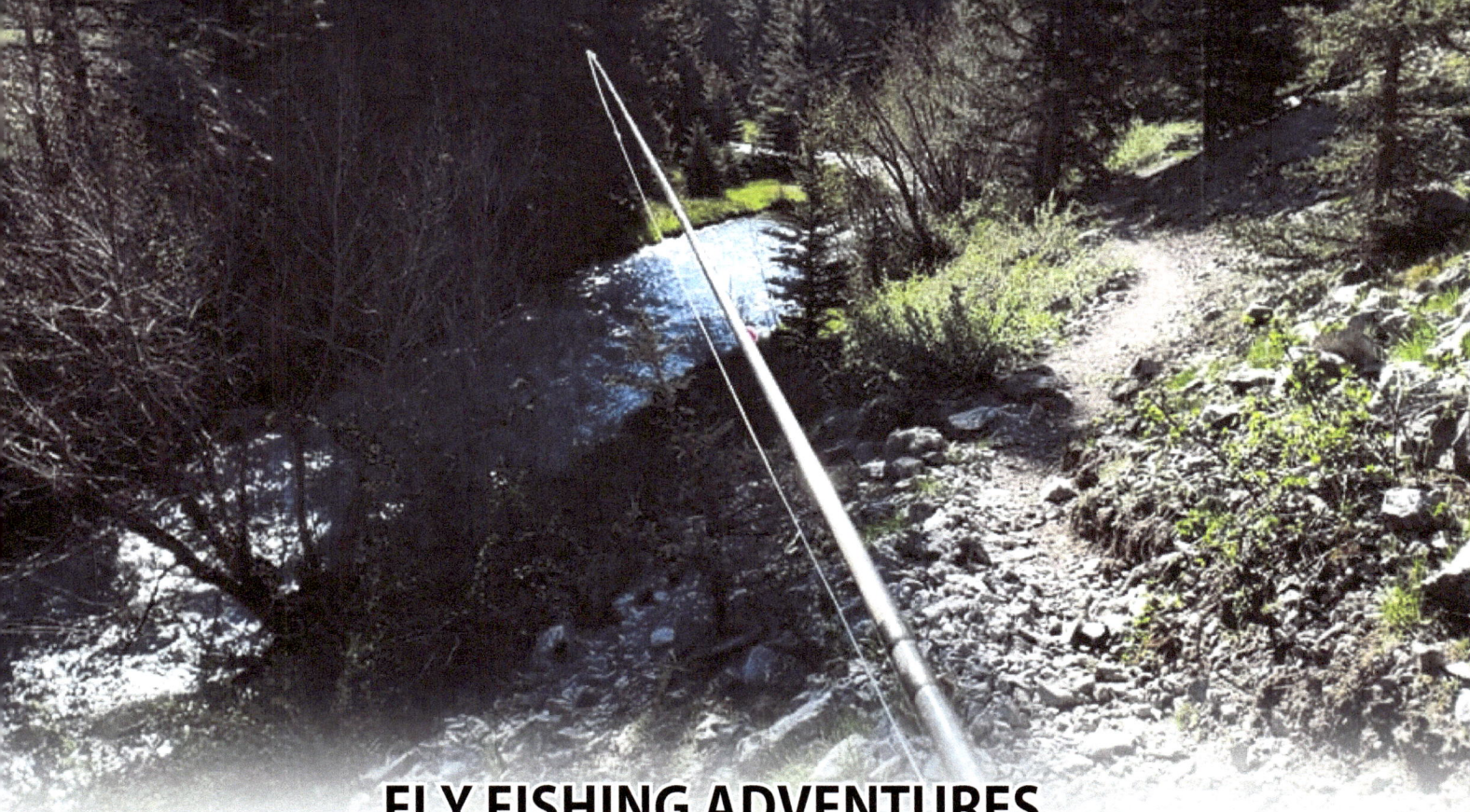

FLY FISHING ADVENTURES

Custom fly fishing expeditions designed for your needs and preferences: with guides, without guides, helicopter runs, fishing lodges, gourmet cooking, cold beverages, fish stories galore. I work fly fishing around your agenda – beginners, advanced, family, corporate groups. Group sizes 2 – 10 people. Subscribe to Fly Fish Mindset email list. You will be informed of pending trips and ongoing fly fishing tips. Subscribe @flyfishmindset.com

Below is my annual fly fishing agenda, subject to change as clients book fishing expeditions.

August 2019	–	Conejos River, Los Pinos River
September 2019	–	Animas River, Pecos River, San Juan River
October 2019	–	Rio Grande River, San Juan River
November 2019	–	Lake Baccarac, Sinaloa, Mexico
December 2019	–	San Juan River
January 2020	–	Belize

February 2020	–	Costa Rica
March 2020	–	San Juan River
April 2020	–	open, based on spring runoff
May 2020	–	open, based on spring runoff
June 2020	–	Arkansas River, Costilla Creek, Conejos River
July 2020	–	Animas River, Rio Grande River, Gunnison River, Soldatna, AK
August 2020	–	Firehole River, Maddison River, WY
September 2020	–	Fort Smith, MT
October 2020	–	Green River, UT
November 2020	–	Chicolete, TX
December 2020	–	Bariloche and Fjords, Argentina

My Current Bucket List

Where I desire to fly fish in the future, 2020 and beyond.

Alaska	–	Tongass National Forrest
Idaho	–	Henry's Fork, Salmon River, Snake River
Oregon	–	Umpqua River, Metolius River
Utah	–	Green River
Vermont	–	Battenkill River
Wyoming	–	Firehole River, Maddison River
Australia	–	Tasmania Central Highlands
New Zealand	–	South Island & North Island
England & Scotland		
Spain	–	Peralejos de las Truchas
Argentina	–	Bariloche, Corrientes, Tierra del Fuego
Brazil	–	Rio Negro, peacock bass
Chile	–	Fjords – Rio Cisnes
Costa Rica	–	tarpon, sailfish
Cuba	–	tarpon
Christmas Island, Pacific Ocean	–	January 2021

Photo Credits

All images © Anthony Atwell, Jr unless otherwise noted:
Front Cover & Page 7 © Adventure Photo/iStock
Pages 1-3 © Siarhei Nosyreu/Adobe Stock
Page 5 © Vidar Nordli-Mathisen/unsplash.com
Page 6 © Lane Erickson/123RF Stock Photo
Page 10 © Adventure Photo/Getty Images
Page 11 © Vito Alfano/unsplash.com
Page 14 © Henry Fraczek/unsplash.com
Pages 15 & 28 © goodluz/123RF Stock Photo
Page 16 © Shea Rouda/unsplash.com
Page 17 © Nicolette/Adobe Stock
Page 18 © Gavin Van Wagoner/unsplash.com
Page 20 licensed by piqsels.com Creative Commons Zero
Page 21 © pastorscott/iStock
Pages 23 & 26 © Vitali Valasevich/shutterstock
Page 24 © Sandra Cunningham/shutterstock
Page 25 © marc phillips/unsplash.com
Page 29 © Sayan Nath/unsplash.com
Page 31 © goodluz/shutterstock
Page 32 © Parilov/Adobe Stock
Page 34 © Daniel Vincek/Adobe Stock
Page 36 © Lukas Gojda/shutterstock

www.ingramcontent.com/pod-product-compliance
Lightning Source LLC
Chambersburg PA
CBHW060823090426

42738CB00002B/83